A Useful Guide
for
English Speakers
Wanting to Communicate
in
French

An 'English' and 'French'
Word Dictionary
comprised of over
2,339
English words
and their equivalent
French counterparts
that are mostly
spelled, pronounced, and mean
the same thing!

RoseDog Books
585 Alpha Drive
Suite 103
Pittsburgh, PA 15238
Visit our website at *www.rosedogbookstore.com*

ISBN: 978-1-4349-6572-0
eISBN: 978-1-4349-6526-3

Introduction

France, along with its language, has been an integral part of the American experience since before we Americans achieved independence from England. Since the late 18th Century the social elite within the American colonies insisted that their progenies achieved fluency in the French language. This demand extended well into the 20th Century in the guise of "Touring the Continent" prior to being accepted into the circle of American Social Society. Regretfully, this requirement was eliminated by the mid-20th Century. Today, one can attain social prominence in American Society without even being grammatically proficient and or fluent in English!

In the early 1960's I could be considered a member of this cadre. My only regret since has been that once opting to take French 101 at the College of Marin in California that after only 6 weeks of instruction I was faced with a decision of continuing with French 101 or pursuing a professional career. Despite my professional paths that have included senior positions in Belgium, and 8 years of retirement in France, I can't profess to claim that I've attained fluency in the French language. However, during my tenure in these countries, I have noted some interesting and helpful facts that might take some of the pain and doubt associated with acquiring a level of survival when dealing with native French speakers.

This 'Guide' should not be considered a substitute for attaining fluency in the French language. Since 1635 the Académie Française has dictated the rules governing the use of French grammar and speech. Similar to Latin, tense and gender references will impact on the spelling of French words. Then, of course, differences in pronunciation of French words, based on its alphabet's 'phonics' are to be considered. Ergo, it is recommended that some practice of the French alphabet and key French phrases be employed. Still, while a correct pronunciation of each French word is not essential (most native French speakers will comprehend what you're trying to say) facility in using the key French 'phrases' highlighted on the following pages will prove essential when attempting to communicate in French.

Bonne Chance
(Good Luck)

The French Alphabet

A	B	C	D	E
(ah)	(bay)	(say)	(day)	(euh)

F	G	H	I	J
(eef)	(jay)	(ash)	(eee)	(gee)

K	L	M	N	O
(kah)	(el)	(em)	(en)	(oh)

P	Q	R	S	T
(pay)	(que)	(air)	(ess)	(tey)

U	V	W	X	Y
(oou)	(vay)	(doubla vay)	(ex)	(e-grek)

Z
(zet)

Observations of Importance and Interest

Whenever attempting to communicate in a language which is not your native-tongue it's essential to memorize a few key phrases. The liberal use of the following phrases and words will go a long way in assuring that the person you are attempting to communicate with will take the time, in most cases, to comprehend what you are attempting to say. In this regard, please note the following phrases. I assure you, liberal use of such phrases and words, especially when attempting to communicate in French, will prove highly beneficial and rewarding:

IS THERE   A (-select a noun subject-)   NEAR HERE?
Y-A-T-IL   UN (-select a noun subject-)   PRES D'ICI ?
(eee-ah-till) (oon) (-select a noun subject-)   (pray) (deesea) ?

THANK YOU VERY MUCH
MERCI BEAUCOUP
(mare-sea) (boo-coo)

THANKS
MERCI
(mare-sea)

PLEASE
S'IL VOUS PLAIT
(seal-voo-play)

Key Words of Importance
and their English prounciations and examples of use

WHO – QUI (Pronounced: KEY)
Ex: who are you? Qui êtes -vous?
(key et-vou?)

WHAT – QUOI (Pronounced: KWAH)
Ex: what do you need? De quoi avez-vous besoin?
(du kwah avey-vou beeswan?)

WHEN – QUAND (Pronounced: KON)
Ex: When do we arrive? Quand arrivons-nous?
(kon arrivon-new?)

WHERE – OU (Pronounced: OOO)
Ex: Where is the (noun of choice)?
(Ou est le (noun of choice)?

WHY – POURQUOI (Pronounced: POR-KWA)
Ex: Why go to a (noun of choice) now?
Pourquoi aller au (noun of choice) mainatenant?
(pourquoi alley ou (noun of choice) men-tin-ont?)

Section One

American English includes 2,339 words that are spelled, pronounced, and mean the same as their French counterparts. In this Section are 1,833 'English' words that are spelled, mean, and are, essentially, pronounced the same as their French counterparts. The Académie Française insists on adding various accents to some of these words to be assured the proper pronunciation emphasis is achieved. However, the user should not be dismayed by these 'accents'. Pronounce the word as if they weren't there. An obliging 'native' French speaker will surely comprehend your meaning and, no doubt, correct your pronunciation error. For reference purposes these French words are indicated with an 'asterisk' (*). Words marked with an (+) indicate that while the word's meaning is essentially the same in both English and French, the French usage has 'multiple' meanings. Ergo, the user should use them with caution.

A

English	French
abandon	abandon
abdication	abdication
abdomen	abdomen
abject	abject
abominable	abominable
abomination	abomination
abrogation	abrogation
absence	absence
absent	absent
absinthe	absinthe
absolution	absolution
abstinence	abstinence
abstraction	abstraction
abuse	abuse
accent	accent
accessible	accessible
accident	accident
acclaim	acclame
accord	accord
accusation	accusation
accuse	accuse
acetate	acétate *
acne	acné *
acre	acre
action	action
acupuncture	acupuncture
adage	adage
addition	addition
adequate	adéquate *

adherence	adhérence *
adhesion	adhésion *
adjacent	adjacent
adjective	adjective
adjudication	adjudication
administration	administration
admirable	admirable
admission	admission
adolescence	adolescence
adorable	adorable
adroit	adroit
aerodrome	aérodrome
aerosol	aérosol *
affectation	affectation
affection	affection
affiliation	affiliation
affliction	affliction
affront	affront
age	âge *
agenda	agenda
agent	agent
agile	agile
agitation	agitation
air	air
album	album
alias	alias
alibi	alibi
alienation	aliénation *
allegation	allégation *
alligator	alligator
allocation	allocation
allure	allure

allusion	allusion
alphabet	alphabet
altitude	altitude
amateur	amateur
ambiance	ambiance
amble	amble
ambulance	ambulance
amen	amen
amoral	amoral
amour	amour
ampere	ampère *
amphitheatre	amphithéâtre *
ample	ample
amplifier	amplifier
amusement	amusement
angle	angle
anglican	anglican
animal	animal
animation	animation
anis	anis
antique	antique
aperitif	apéritif *
apocalypse	apocalypse
apogee	apogée *
apostrophe	apostrophe *
appearance	apparence *
apparent	apparent
appellation	appellation
appetit	appétit *
applicable	applicable
application	application
apposition	apposition

approximation	approximation
aptitude	aptitude
aquaplane	aquaplane
aquarium	aquarium
arabesque	arabesque
arable	arable
arcade	arcade
ardent	ardent
argument	argument
armistice	armistice
arrangement	arrangement
arrogance	arrogance
arsenic	arsenic
art	art
article	article
artisan	artisan
aspect	aspect
aspic	aspic
assassin	assassin
assemble	assemble
assertion	assertion
assistance	assistance
association	association
assurance	assurance
assure	assure
atlas	atlas
atmosphere	atmosphère *
atoll	atoll
attention	attention
attraction	attraction
audience	audience
audition	audition

automation	automation
automobile	automobile
avalanche	avalanche
avenue	avenue
aversion	aversion
aviation	aviation
axis	axis
azure	azure

B

English	French
bah	bah
balance	balance
ballade	ballade
ballast	ballast
ballet	ballet
balustrade	balustrade
banal	banal
bandage	bandage
band	band
bandit	bandit
bang	bang
banjo	banjo
banquet	banquet
bar	bar
barbecue	barbecue
bard	bard
baron	baron
base	base
baseball	baseball
basketball	basketball
bastion	bastion
baton	bâton *
bazooka	bazooka
beau	beau
Bedouin	Bédouin*
beige	beige
belle	belle
belligerence	belligérance *
benediction	bénédiction *

benzene	benzène *
beret	béret *
bible	bible
bibliographies	bibliographies
biceps	biceps
bidet	bidet
bigot	bigot
bikini	bikini
billiards	billards
billion	billion
biscuit	biscuit
bismuth	bismuth
bistro	bistro
bivouac	bivouac
bizarre	bizarre
blame	blâme *
blizzard	blizzard
bloc	bloc
blockhouse	block house
blond	blond
blouse	blouse
blues	blues
bluff	bluff
boa	boa
bolero	boléro *
boulevard	boulevard
bonnet	bonnet
buddha	buddha
boudoir	boudoir
bouquet	bouquet
bowling	bowling
box	box

bracelet	bracelet
brave	brave
bravo	bravo
Breton	Breton
brick-a-brac	brick-a-brac
bride	bride
bridge	bridge
brigade	brigade
brilliant	brillant
bronze	bronze
brouhaha	brouhaha
buffet	buffet
buffoon	bouffon*
bulldozer	bulldozer
bulletin	bulletin
bungalow	bungalow
bureau	bureau
burlesque	burlesque

C

English	French
cabaret	cabaret
cabinet	cabinet
cable	câble *
cocoa	cacao *
cactus	cactus
cadence	cadence
cadet	cadet
cadre	cadre
café	café
cage	cage
caisson	caisson
cake	cake +
calcium	calcium
calorie	calorie
camera	camera
camp	camp
campus	campus
Canada	Canada
canal	canal
canapé	canapé
cancer	cancer
candelabra	candélabre *
canoe	canoë *
capable	capable
capital	capital
caprice	caprice
capsule	capsule
carafe	carafe
caramel	caramel

carat	carat
cardinal	cardinal
caricature	caricature
carnage	carnage
carte	carte
cartilage	cartilage
carton	carton
cascade	cascade
casserole	casserole +
caste	caste
catalogue	catalogue
cause	cause
cavalcade	cavalcade
cavalier	cavalier
cave	cave
caviar	caviar
cede	cède *
cellophane	cellophane
celluloid	celluloïd *
centigrade	centigrade
centrifuge	centrifuge
certain	certain
cervical	cervical
chagrin	chagrin
chalet	chalet
challenge	challenge
chamois	chamois
champion	champion
change	change +
chant	chant +
chaos	chaos
chapeau	chapeau

charade	charade
chariot	chariot
charitable	charitable
charlatan	charlatan
charter	charter +
chaste	chaste
chateau	château *
chauffeur	chauffeur
chemise	chemise +
chevron	chevron
chic	chic
chips	chips +
cholera	cholera
cholesterol	cholestérol *
choral	choral
chorus	chorus +
Christ	Christ
chromosome	chromosome
cinema	cinéma *
circumference	circonférence *
circumstance	circonstance *
clarion	clairon
clairvoyance	clairvoyance
clandestine	clandestine
clause	clause
clementine	clémentine *
cliché	cliché
client	client
clown	clown
club	club
cobalt	cobalt
cobra	cobra

cocaine	cocaïne *
code	code
coefficient	coefficient
cognac	cognac
cohabitation	cohabitation
coherent	cohérent *
cohesion	cohésion *
coiffeur	coiffeur
coincidence	coïncidence *
coke	coke
colonel	colonel
coma	coma
combat	combat
combustible	combustible
commandant	commandant
commando	commando
commerce	commerce
commission	commission
commotion	commotion
commune	commune
communication	communication
compartment	compartiment
compassion	compassion
compatible	compatible
competence	compétence *
competition	compétition *
complement	complément *
complete	complet O *
complication	complication
compliment	compliment
composite	composite
comprehensible	compréhensible *

compression	compression
conception	conception
concert	concert
concession	concession
concierge	concierge
conclave	conclave
conference	conférence *
confession	confession
confetti	confetti
confidence	confidence
configuration	configuration
Congo	Congo
conscience	conscience
consecration	consécration *
consequence	conséquence *
conserve	conserve
considerable	considérable *
consideration	considération *
consistence	consistance + *
consortium	consortium
constant	constant
constellation	constellation
consternation	consternation
construction	construction +
consul	consul
contact	contact
contagion	contagion
content	content
continent	continent
contraception	contraception
contradiction	contradiction
convalescence	convalescence

convection	convection
conversation	conversation
conviction	conviction
cornet	cornet
corps	corps
corpulence	corpulence
correct	correct
correlation	corrélation *
correspondence	correspondance
corridor	corridor
corruption	corruption
corset	corset
corvette	corvette
cosmos	cosmos
costume	costume +
couple	couple
coupon	coupon
courage	courage
course	course +
court	court +
cousin	cousin
coyote	coyote
credo	credo
Creole	Créole *
crepe	crêpe + *
crescendo	crescendo
crime	crime +
crochet	crochet +
croissant	croissant +
cru	cru +
cruel	cruel
Cuba	Cuba

cube	cube
cuisine	cuisine +
cure	cure +
cycle	cycle
cyclone	cyclone

D

English	French
dahlia	dahlia
dame	dame
damnation	damnation
danger	danger
date	date
debacle	débâcle*
debate	débâte*
debit	débit*
debris	débris*
debut	début*
decadence	décadence*
decanter	décanter*
decision	décision*
declaration	déclaration*
declare	déclare*
decline	décline*
decode	décode*
decompose	décompose*
deduction	déduction*
deductible	déductible*
defective	défective*
defense	défense*
defensive	défensive*
deficit	déficit*
definition	définition*
deflation	déflation*
déjà vu	déjà vu
delegation	délégation*
deliberation	délibération*

delicate	délicate*
delta	delta
demi	demi
demon	démon*
demonstration	démonstration*
deodorant	déodorant*
department	département*
depose	dépose*
deplore	déplore*
depot	dépôt*
depravation	dépravation*
depression	dépression*
derision	dérision*
derivation	dérivation*
derrick	derrick
derriere	derrière*
desire	désire*
description	description
desert	désert*
designation	désignation*
desire	désire*
dessert	dessert
destination	destination
destructible	destructible
detail	détail*
detective	détective*
détente	détente *
detention	détention *
detergent	détergent *
determine	détermine *
detour	détour *
devalue	dévalue *

deviation	déviation *
diagonal	diagonal
dialogue	dialogue
diatribe	diatribe
diesel	diesel
difference	différence *
different	différent *
digital	digital
digression	digression
diligence	diligence
dimension	dimension
dine	dine
diocese	diocèse *
direction	direction
disadvantage	désavantage *
disciple	disciple
discipline	discipline
discretion	discrétion *
disgrace	disgrâce *
disparate	disparate
disperse	disperse
disproportion	disproportion
dissection	dissection
dissidence	dissidence
dissident	dissident
dissolution	dissolution
dissonance	dissonance
dissuade	dissuade
distance	distance
distiller	distiller
distinct	distinct
distraction	distraction

district	district
divan	divan
diverge	diverge
diverse	diverse
diversion	diversion
divorce	divorce
docile	docile
dock	dock
doctrine	doctrine
document	document
doge	doge
dollar	dollar
dome	dôme *
dope	dope
dorsal	dorsal
dose	dose
double	double
dune	dune
duodenum	duodénum *
dupe	dupe
duplex	duplex
durable	durable
dynamite	dynamite
dynamo	dynamo

E

English	French
echo	écho *
eclipse	éclipse *
Eden	Eden
education	éducation *
effervescence	effervescence
effort	effort
élan	élan +
electrode	électrode *
electron	électron *
elegant	élégant *
element	élément *
elevation	élévation *
eligible	éligible *
elite	élite *
embargo	embargo
eminence	éminence *
emir	émir *
emission	émission *
emotion	émotion *
empire	empire
emulsion	émulsion
enclave	enclave
encore	encore
encourage	encourage
engagement	engagement
ensemble	ensemble
entrée	entrée
envoi	envoi
epee	épée *

epilogue	épilogue *
epic	épic *
episode	épisode *
ersatz	ersatz
erudite	érudite*
eruption	éruption *
escalope	escalope
escargot	escargot
escort	escort
essence	essence
essential	essential
et cetera	et cetera
ether	éther *
etiquette	étiquette *
eucalyptus	eucalyptus
Europe	Europe
Eurovision	Eurovision
evidence	évidence *
evocation	évocation *
exact	exact
exaction	exaction
examine	examine
excavation	excavation
excellence	excellence
excrement	excrément *
excretion	excrétion *
excursion	excursion
exempt	exempt
exile	exile
expansion	expansion
expedient	expédient *
expert	expert

exploit	exploit
exploration	exploration
export	export
express	express
expression	expression
extension	extension
extinction	extinction
extra	extra
extraction	extraction
extravagance	extravagance
extreme	extrême *
exuberance	exubérance *

F

English	French
façade	façade *
face	face
facture	facture
fade	fade
fanfare	fanfare
farce	farce
fatal	fatal
fatigue	fatigue
federal	fédéral *
federation	fédération *
felon	félon *
ferry	ferry
fertile	fertile
fervent	fervent
festival	festival
festivities	festivités *
fiancé	fiancé
fiasco	fiasco
figure	figure
figurine	figurine
film	film
final	final
finance	finance
finesse	finesse
fission	fission
fjord	fjord
flagrant	flagrant
flan	flan
flash	flash

flexible	flexible
flirt	flirt
floral	floral
folklore	folklore
fondue	fondue +
football	football +
force	force +
forceps	forceps
fox terrier	fox terrier
foyer	foyer +
fraction	fraction
fracture	fracture
fragile	fragile
fragment	fragment
franchise	franchise +
freezer	freezer
frequent	fréquent*
friction	friction +
frugal	frugal
fruit	fruit
fuel	fuel
fusion	fusion

G

English	French
gabardine	gabardine
gadget	gadget
gag	gag
gaga	gaga
gallon	gallon
gang	gang
gangrene	gangrène *
gangster	gangster
garage	garage
garcon	garçon *
gazette	gazette
gendarme	gendarme
gene	gène *
general	général *
genital	génital*
genocide	génocide *
geranium	géranium *
gestation	gestation
geyser	geyser
ghetto	ghetto
gigolo	gigolo
gin	gin
global	global
glucose	glucose
gnome	gnome
golf	golf
gong	gong
gorge	gorge
gourmand	gourmand

grace	grâce *
gradation	gradation
grade	grade +
graffiti	graffiti
grammatical	grammatical
grand	grand
grandeur	grandeur
grandiose	grandiose
granite	granite
granule	granule
graphite	graphite
gratis	gratis
gratitude	gratitude
grave	grave
grimace	grimace
grog	grog
grotesque	grotesque
gruyere	gruyère *
guide	guide
guillotine	guillotine
gym	gym
gyroscope	gyroscope

H

English	French
habitable	habitable
habitat	habitat
haddock	haddock
hall	hall
hallucination	hallucination
halo	halo
handball	handball
handicap	handicap
harangue	harangue
harem	harem
harmonica	harmonica
hectare	hectare
helium	hélium
hemisphere	hémisphère *
heritage	héritage *
heroine	héroïne *
heron	héron *
hero	héro *
hockey	hockey
hold-up	hold-up
horde	horde
hormone	hormone
horoscope	horoscope
horrible	horrible
hostile	hostile
hotel	hôtel *
humble	humble
humus	humus
hydrofoil	hydrofoil
hygiene	hygiène
hyper	hyper
hypo	hypo

I

English	French
iceberg	iceberg
icône	icône *
ideal	idéal
identifiable	identifiable
idiot	idiot
igloo	igloo
ignorance	ignorance
illegal	illégal *
illusion	illusion
image	image
imbecile	imbécile*
imbroglio	imbroglio
immemorial	immémorial *
immense	immense
imminence	imminence
immobile	immobile
impact	impact
impalpable	impalpable
impasse	impasse
impatience	impatience
impenetrable	impénétrable *
imperceptible	imperceptible
imperfection	imperfection
imperial	impérial*
impermeable	imperméable *
impertinence	impertinence
imperturbable	imperturbable
implacable	implacable
implication	implication

imponderable	impondérable *
importance	importance
impotent	impotent
impregnation	imprégnation *
imprecise	imprécise
impression	impression
impressionable	impressionnable
impromptu	impromptu
imprudent	imprudent
imprudence	imprudence
inaccessible	inaccessible
inadequate	inadéquate *
inadmissible	inadmissible
inalienable	inaliénable *
inapplicable	inapplicable
inattention	inattention
inaudible	inaudible
incalculable	incalculable
incandescence	incandescence
incantation	incantation
incapable	incapable
incessant	incessant
incidence	incidence
incident	incident
incognito	incognito
incoherent	incohérent *
incombustible	incombustible
incomparable	incomparable
inconsolable	inconsolable
incontinence	incontinence
inconvenient	inconvénient * +
incorrect	incorrect

incorrigible	incorrigible
incorruptible	incorruptible
incurable	incurable
indecent	indécent *
indelicate	indélicate *
indentation	indentation
independence	indépendance *
index	index
indifference	indifférence *
indigestion	indigestion
indigo	indigo
indirect	indirect
indispensable	indispensable
indissoluble	indissoluble
indistinct	indistinct
induction	induction
indulgent	indulgent
ineffable	ineffable
inestimable	inestimable
inevitable	inévitable *
inexact	inexact
inexcusable	inexcusable
inexperience	inexpérience *
inexplicable	inexplicable
infallible	infaillible
infernal	infernal
infertile	infertile
inflammable	inflammable
inflation	inflation
inflexible	inflexible
inflexion	inflexion
influence	influence

influx	influx
information	information
infraction	infraction
infrastructure	infrastructure
ingredient	ingrédient *
inherent	inhérent*
initial	initial
innocent	innocent
inopportune	inopportune
insatiable	insatiable
inscription	inscription
insensible	insensible
inseparable	inséparable *
insoluble	insoluble
installation	installation
instance	instance
instigation	instigation
instinct	instinct
instruction	instruction
instrument	instrument
insubordination	insubordination
insurmountable	insurmontable
insurrection	insurrection
intact	intact
integral	intégral *
intellect	intellect
intelligence	intelligence
intelligible	intelligible
intense	intense
intention	intention
interaction	interaction
interchangeable	interchangeable
interdependence	interdépendance *

interference	interférence *
interjection	interjection
interlude	interlude
intermittent	intermittent
international	international
interrogation	interrogation
intersection	intersection
interview	interview
intolerable	intolérable *
intolerance	intolérance *
intolerant	intolérant *
intonation	intonation
intuition	intuition
invariable	invariable
invasion	invasion
invective	invective
investigation	investigation
invincible	invincible
inviolable	inviolable
invisible	invisible
invocation	invocation
invulnerable	invulnérable *
ion	ion
irascible	irascible
irrefutable	irréfutable *
irreparable	irréparable *
irrepressible	irrépressible *
irresistible	irrésistible *
irreversible	irréversible *
irrevocable	irrévocable *
irruption	irruption
isotope	isotope
issue	issue
itinerant	itinérant *

J

English	French
jade	jade
jaguar	jaguar
jargon	jargon
jazz	jazz
jeep	jeep
jersey	jersey
Jesus	Jésus *
jet	jet
jockey	jockey
joker	joker
journal	journal
jovial	jovial
judo	judo
jungle	jungle
junior	junior
jury	jury
justice	justice
jute	jute

K

English	French
kaleidoscope	kaléidoscope *
kamikaze	kamikaze
kapok	kapok
karate	karaté *
kayak	kayak
kepi	képi *
kerosene	kérosène *
kilo	kilo
kimono	kimono
kirsch	kirsch
kiwi	kiwi
knock-out	knock-out
koala	koala

L

English	French
lama	lama
lamentable	lamentable
lance	lance
laps	laps
lard	lard +
large	large
largesse	largesse +
larynx	larynx
laser	laser
lasso	lasso
latent	latent
lateral	latéral *
latex	latex
Latin	Latin
latitude	latitude
lecture	lecture
legal	légal *
legation	légation *
legion	légion *
legislation	législation *
leopard	léopard *
liaison	liaison
libation	libation
liberal	libéral *
libertine	libertine
lichen	lichen
lieutenant	lieutenant
linoleum	linoléum *
liqueur	liqueur

lobe	lobe
local	local +
location	location +
locomotion	locomotion
locomotive	locomotive
locution	locution
loggia	loggia
long	long +
longitude	longitude
lotion	lotion
lotus	lotus
loyal	loyal
luge	luge
lumbago	lumbago
lunch	lunch
luxuriance	luxuriance
lynx	lynx

M

English	French
macabre	macabre
macadam	macadam
macaroni	macaroni
mach	mach
machine	machine +
macro	macro
mademoiselle	mademoiselle
magazine	magazine
magma	magma
magnesium	magnésium *
magneto	magnéto *
magnificence	magnificence
male	male
malice	malice
malleable	malléable *
malnutrition	malnutrition
malt	malt
mandarin	mandarin +
mannequin	mannequin +
manufacture	manufacture
marathon	marathon
marauder	marauder
margarine	margarine
marguerite	marguerite
marijuana	marijuana
marine	marine +
marital	marital
maritime	maritime +
marmalade	marmelade

martial	martial
martyr	martyr
masculine	masculine
massacre	massacre
mass media	mass media
match	match
matrimonial	matrimonial
maxi	maxi
maximum	maximum
mayonnaise	mayonnaise
medallion	médaillon *
mediation	médiation *
medieval	médiéval *
mediocre	médiocre *
meditation	méditation *
meeting	meeting +
mega	méga *
melon	melon
membrane	membrane
memoire	mémoire * +
memorable	mémorable *
menace	menace
menagerie	ménagerie *
menopause	ménopause *
menstruation	menstruation
mental	mental
mention	mention
menu	menu +
meringue	meringue
mess	mess
message	message
metal	métal

methane	méthane *
metronome	métronome *
mica	mica
microbe	microbe
micron	micron
microphone	microphone
microscope	microscope
migraine	migraine
migration	migration
millet	millet
million	million
mime	mime
mimosa	mimosa
mine	mine +
mineral	minéral *
mini	mini
miniature	miniature
minimum	minimum
minuscule	minuscule
minute	minute
miracle	miracle
mirage	mirage
missile	missile
mission	mission
missive	missive
mixture	mixture
mobile	mobile
moccasin	mocassin
mode	mode +
module	module
modulation	modulation
moment	moment

monochrome	monochrome
monocle	monocle
monologue	monologue
montage	montage
monument	monument
moral	moral
morgue	morgue
morose	morose
morphine	morphine
motel	motel
motif	motif
motion	motion
moustache	moustache
multinational	multinational
multiple	multiple +
multitude	multitude
municipal	municipal
Muscat	Muscat
muscle	muscle
muse	muse

N

English	French
napalm	napalm
nation	nation
nature	nature +
naval	naval
Nazi	Nazi
nectar	nectar
neon	néon *
neophyte	néophyte *
net	net
niche	niche
nickel	nickel
nicotine	nicotine
niece	nièce *
nitrate	nitrate
noble	noble
noel	noël *
noir	noir
nomenclature	nomenclature
nonchalance	nonchalance
normal	normal
notable	notable
note	note +
notation	notation +
notion	notion
nougat	nougat
nouveau	nouveau
novice	novice
nuance	nuance +
nuptial	nuptial
nutrition	nutrition
nylon	nylon

O

English	French
oasis	oasis
obese	obese
object	objet
objection	objection
obligation	obligation
oblique	oblique
oblong	oblong
obscene	obscène *
obscure	obscure
observance	observance
observation	observation
obsession	obsession
obstacle	obstacle
ostentation	ostentation
obtuse	obtuse
occasion	occasion
occurrence	occurrence
ocean	océan *
octane	octane
octave	octave
ode	ode
office	office
ogre	ogre
olive	olive
omnibus	omnibus
omnipotence	omnipotence
omnipresent	omniprésent *
omniscient	omniscient
onyx	onyx

opaque	opaque
opera	opéra *
opinion	opinion
opium	opium
opportune	opportune
opposition	opposition
optimum	optimum
option	option
opulent	opulent
opulence	opulence
oracle	oracle
oral	oral
orange	orange
oratorio	oratorio
ordinal	ordinal
orient	orient
orientation	orientation
orifice	orifice
original	original
Oscar	Oscar
ostentation	ostentation
outrage	outrage
ovation	ovation
ozone	ozone

P

English	French
page	page +
pale	pale
palette	palette
palpitation	palpitation
pancreas	pancréas *
panorama	panorama
pantheon	panthéon *
pantomime	pantomime
papa	papa
parquet	parquet +
parachute	parachute
parade	parade
parapet	parapet
paraphrase	paraphrase
parasite	parasite
parasol	parasol
pardon	pardon
parent	parent
parking	parking
parquet	parquet +
part	part
partial	partial
partisan	partisan
partition	partition
passage	passage
passion	passion
pastel	pastel
pastille	pastille
pastoral	pastoral

patisserie	pâtisserie *
patois	patois
patron	patron
pause	pause
pave	pave
pedigree	pedigree
pelican	pélican *
penal	pénal *
penchant	penchant
pendant	pendant +
penitence	pénitence *
pension	pension
perception	perception
perfection	perfection
performance	performance
perfusion	perfusion
peril	péril *
periscope	périscope *
permanence	permanence
permeable	perméable *
perseverance	persévérance *
personnel	personnel +
perspective	perspective
persuade	persuade *
pertinent	pertinent
perverse	perverse
petite	petite
petition	pétition *
pharynx	pharynx
phase	phase
phosphate	phosphate
photo	photo

phrase	phrase
physique	physique
piano	piano
piece	pièce *
pigeon	pigeon
pigment	pigment
pile	pile
ping pong	ping pong
pipe	pipe
pipe-line	pipeline
pirate	pirate
pirouette	pirouette
piston	piston
pivot	pivot
place	place +
plan	plan +
plantation	plantation
plaque	plaque
plasma	plasma
plate	plate +
plateau	plateau
platitude	platitude
plausible	plausible
plebiscite	plébiscite
plexiglas	plexiglas
plume	plume +
plutonium	plutonium
podium	podium
point	point +
poison	poison +
poker	poker
police	police

polio	polio
polka	polka
pollen	pollen
polo	polo +
polychrome	polychrome
polyester	polyester
polyvalent	polyvalent
pop	pop
population	population
port	port
portrait	portrait
pose	pose
position	position +
possession	possession
possible	possible
poster	poster +
posture	posture
pot	pot +
potable	potable
potion	potion
prairie	prairie
praline	praline
precaution	précaution *
precede	précède *
precedence	preseance *
precise	précise *
precision	précision *
prediction	prédiction *
predilection	prédilection *
predispose	prédispose *
preeminence	prééminence *
preexist	préexiste *

prefect	préfet *
prefecture	préfecture *
prejudice	préjudice * +
prelude	prélude *
premature	primature
premier	premier +
premonition	prémonition *
prepare	prépare * +
preparation	préparation *
preponderance	prépondérance *
preposition	préposition *
prerogative	prérogative *
presence	présence *
present	présent * +
presentation	présentation *
president	président *
pressing	pressing +
prestige	prestige
presuppose	présuppose *
prime	prime +
primordial	primordial
principal	principal
prison	prison
privilege	privilège *
probable	probable
procedure	procédure *
procession	procession
profession	profession
profit	profit
profusion	profusion
projectile	projectile
projection	projection

proliferation	prolifération *
prologue	prologue
promenade	promenade +
promotion	promotion +
prompt	prompt
propane	propane
proportion	proportion
prose	prose
prospectus	prospectus
prostate	prostate
prostration	prostration
protection	protection
protestant	protestant
prototype	prototype
protuberance	protubérance *
providence	providence
province	province
provincial	provincial
provision	provision +
prude	prude
prudent	prudent
prune	prune
pseudo	pseudo
public	public +
publication	publication
puma	puma
puree	purée *
purge	purge
putsch	putsch
puzzle	puzzle
python	python

Q

English	French
quadruple	quadruple
qualification	qualification
quartette	quartette
quartz	quartz
quatrain	quatrain
question	question
quinine	quinine
quintessence	quintessence
quotient	quotient

R

English	French
race	race +
racial	racial
radar	radar
radiation	radiation
radical	radical
radio	radio
radium	radium
rage	rage
raid	raid +
rail	rail
raisin	raisin
rapport	rapport
rat	rat +
ration	ration
ravage	ravage
reaction	réaction *
recent	récent *
reception	réception *
recession	récession *
recharge	recharge
recital	récital *
recluse	recluse
recommendation	recommandation
recompense	récompense *
reconstitution	reconstitution
record	record
recreation	récréation *
rectangle	rectangle
rectitude	rectitude

redemption	rédemption *
reduction	réduction *
reference	référence *
referendum	référendum *
refrain	refrain
refuge	refuge
regard	regard +
regent	régent *
regime	régime *
regiment	régiment *
region	région *
regret	regret
regulation	régulation *
rehabilitation	réhabilitation *
relation	relation
relegation	relégation *
relief	relief +
religion	religion
remission	rémission *
renaissance	renaissance
renovation	rénovation *
reporter	reporter +
repression	répression *
reprise	reprise +
reptile	reptile
repulsion	répulsion *
reputation	réputation *
requiem	requiem
reservation	réservation *
reserve	réserve *
reservist	réserviste *
resident	résident *

resistance	résistance *
respect	respect
resemble	ressemble
restaurant	restaurant
restriction	restriction
resurrection	résurrection *
retention	rétention *
reticent	réticent *
retrograde	rétrograde *
revenue	revenue
reverence	révérence *
reverend	révérend *
reversible	réversible *
revocation	révocation *
revolution	révolution*
revolver	revolver
rhinoceros	rhinocéros *
rhododendron	rhododendron
rhubarb	rhubarbe *
ridicule	ridicule
ring	ring
rite	rite
rivet	rivet
robe	robe
robot	robot
rock	rock +
role	rôle *
romance	romance +
rose	rose +
rosé	rosé
rosette	rosette
rotation	rotation

rotor	rotor
roulade	roulade
roulette	roulette +
route	route
routine	routine
royal	royal
rude	rude +
rudiment	rudiment
rugby	rugby
rupture	rupture
rural	rural
ruse	ruse
rutabaga	rutabaga
rhythm	rythme *

S

English	French
sabre	sabre
saccharine	saccharine
sachet	sachet
sacrifice	sacrifice
sacrilege	sacrilège *
sacrum	sacrum
safari	safari
sage	sage +
saint	saint +
salami	salami
saline	saline
salon	salon +
salutation	salutation
sanatorium	sanatorium
sanction	sanction
sandwich	sandwich
sans	sans +
sardine	sardine
Satan	Satan
satellite	satellite
satin	satin
satire	satire
satisfaction	satisfaction
sauce	sauce
sauna	sauna
saxophone	saxophone
scalp	scalp
scalpel	scalpel
scandal	scandale*

scenario	scenario
scene	scène *
scission	scission
scooter	scooter
score	score
scorpion	scorpion
scotch	scotch
scout	scout
scribe	scribe
script	script
sec	sec
secession	sécession *
second	second +
secret	secret
section	section
sediment	sédiment *
segment	segment
segregation	ségrégation *
self service	self service
semaphore	sémaphore *
semi	semi +
sensation	sensation
sentence	sentence
sentiment	sentiment
separable	séparable *
separation	séparation *
sequence	séquence *
serenade	sérénade *
serf	serf
series	séries *
sermon	sermon
serpent	serpent

serum	sérum *
servant	servant
service	service +
servile	servile
servitude	servitude
session	session
sever	sévère *
sextant	sextant
Shah	Shah
short	short +
sic	sic
sigma	sigma
signal	signal
signature	signature
silence	silence
silhouette	silhouette
silicone	silicone
simple	simple
simulation	simulation
sinecure	sinécure*
sinus	sinus
siphon	siphon
sire	sire +
site	site +
situation	situation
six	six
sketch	sketch
ski	ski
slalom	slalom
slip	slip +
slogan	slogan
slow	slow +

snack bar	snack bar
snob	snob
sociable	sociable
social	social
socio	socio
soda	soda
sodium	sodium
sofa	sofa
sole	sole
solitude	solitude
solo	solo
solstice	solstice
soluble	soluble
solution	solution
sommelier	sommelier
soprano	soprano
sortie	sortie +
source	source +
souvenir	souvenir +
spatial	spatial
speaker	speaker
special	spécial *
specimen	spécimen *
spectacle	spectacle
sphere	sphère *
sphinx	sphinx
sport	sport
stable	stable
stage	stage
stalactite	stalactite
stalagmite	stalagmite
stand	stand

standard	standard
standing	standing +
star	star +
station	station
statue	statue
stature	stature
stencil	stencil
steno	sténo *
steppe	steppe
stereo	stéréo *
stereotype	stéréotype *
sterile	stérile *
sternum	sternum
stethoscope	stéthoscope *
steward	steward
stock	stock
stop	stop
stratosphere	stratosphère *
strict	strict
strident	strident
structure	structure
studio	studio
style	style
suave	suave
sublime	sublime
subsistence	subsistance
substance	substance
subterfuge	subterfuge
subvention	subvention
subversion	subversion
succession	succession
succinct	succinct

succulent	succulent
suffrage	suffrage
suggestion	suggestion
suite	suite
sultan	sultan
superstition	superstition
superstructure	superstructure
supplement	supplément *
suppliant	suppliant
support	support +
supporter	supporter
suppose	suppose
supreme	suprême*
surcharge	surcharge
surface	surface
surplus	surplus
susceptible	susceptible +
suspect	suspect
suspense	suspense
suspension	suspension +
suture	suture
svelte	svelte
Sycomore	Sycomore
symposium	symposium
synagogue	synagogue
syndrome	syndrome
syphilis	syphilis

T

English	French
tabernacle	tabernacle
table	table
tactile	tactile
talc	talc
talent	talent
talisman	talisman
talon	talon +
tambour	tambour +
tampon	tampon +
tandem	tandem
tangent	tangent
tangible	tangible
tank	tank
tanker	tanker
tapioca	tapioca
taxi	taxi
telecommunications	télécommunications*
telephone	téléphone *
telescope	télescope *
teletype	télétype *
television	télévision *
telex	télex *
temperament	tempérament *
temperance	tempérance *
temperature	température *
temple	temple
temps	temps +
tenant	tenant +
tendance	tendance

tendon	tendon
tennis	tennis
tension	tension
terminus	terminus
termite	termite
terrain	terrain
Terre	Terre
terrible	terrible
terrine	terrine
test	test
testament	testament
textile	textile
texture	texture
theatre	théâtre *
theme	thème *
thermos	thermos
thermostat	thermostat
thorax	thorax
tibia	tibia
ticket	ticket
timbre	timbre *
toast	toast
toboggan	toboggan
tomahawk	tomahawk
tombola	tombola
tome	tome
tonnage	tonnage
torrent	torrent
tort	tort +
torture	torture
toucan	toucan
tour	tour +

tournedos	tournedos
trace	trace
traction	traction
tradition	tradition
train	train
tramway	tramway
transaction	transaction
transcendence	transcendance
transcendent	transcendent
transformer	transformer +
transgression	transgression
transistor	transistor
transit	transit
transition	transition
transparence	transparence
transport	transport
transposition	transposition
transversal	transversal
trapeze	trapèze *
triangle	triangle
tribunal	tribunal
tribune	tribune
tricycle	tricycle
trident	trident
tripe	tripe
triple	triple
triste	triste
trolley-bus	trolleybus
trombone	trombone
trotter	trotter +
troubadour	troubadour
trouble	trouble +

troupe	troupe
trousseau	trousseau
trust	trust
Tsar	Tsar
tuba	tuba
tubercle	tubercule *
tunnel	tunnel
turban	turban
turbine	turbine
turbulent	turbulent
turquoise	turquoise
tutu	tutu
type	type
typhus	typhus

U

English	French
ultimatum	ultimatum
ultra	ultra
union	union
unique	unique
uranium	uranium
urine	urine
usage	usage

V

English	French
vacant	vacant
vaccine	vaccine
vagabond	vagabond +
vain	vain
valet	valet
valise	valise
vampire	vampire
variation	variation
vase	vase
vaseline	vaseline
vassal	vassal
Vatican	Vatican
vaudeville	vaudeville
vendetta	vendetta
vengeance	vengeance
veranda	véranda *
verbal	verbal
verbiage	verbiage
verdict	verdict
vermillion	vermillon
vertical	vertical
vestibule	vestibule
veteran	vétéran *
veto	veto
via	via
vice	vice
vice versa	vice versa
Vietnam	Vietnam
vigilant	vigilant

vignette	vignette
villa	villa
village	village
violent	violent
violet	violet
viral	viral
virus	virus
visa	visa +
visible	visible
vision	vision
vive	vive
vivisection	vivisection
vocal	vocal
vocation	vocation
vogue	vogue
volleyball	volleyball
volt	volt
volume	volume
voyage	voyage

W

English	French
wagon	wagon +
water polo	water polo
watt	watt
weekend	weekend
western	western
whiskey	whiskey

X

English	French
xray	xray
xerox	xerox
xylophone	xylophone

Y

English	French
yacht	yacht
yoga	yoga
yoyo	yoyo

Z

English	French
zebra	zébre
zenith	zénith
zero	zéro
zigzag	zigzag
zinc	zinc
zone	zone
zoo	zoo

Section Two

American English includes an additional 506 words 'borrowed' from the French language that are basically spelled, pronounced, and mean the same as their French counterparts, but with a slightly different ending. For reasons 'unexplained', the Académie Française has an affinity for adding an (e) to some English word endings and (que) to English word's ending in (y). For reference purposes these words are indicated in this section with an 'asterisk' (*). To add to one's angst, on occasion the Académie Française has elected to drop the (e) from a few English words ending in this letter or adding an (e) to its English counterpart. Such words are indicated in this section with the letter (O). The Académie Française, again, insists on adding various 'accents' to many of these words. Still, the user should not be dismayed; in most cases their 'pronunciation' will be close enough that a native French speaker will usually comprehend your meaning.

A

English	French
abscess	abcès *
aborigine	aborigène *
absurd	absurde
accept	accepte *
accordion	accordéon *
acrimony	acrimonie *
acrobat	acrobate *
act	acte *
actor	acteur *
actress	actrice *
actuality	actualité *
affiliation	affiliation
affinity	affinité *
affirmative	affirmatif *
aid	aide *
algebra	algèbre *
alps	alpes
aluminum	aluminium
amulet	amulette *
anagram	anagramme *
analogy	analogie *
analysis	analyse *
anarchy	anarchie *
anatomy	anatomie *
anamosity	anamosite *
annex	annexe *
antenna	antenne *
aorta	aorte *
apology	apologie *

apartment	appartement *
apropos	à-propos *
apt	apte *
arab	arabe *
archeology	archéologie *
architect	architecte *
aristocrat	aristocrate *
arithmetic	arithmétique *
arm	arme *
artificial	artificiel *
artillery	artillerie *
assumption	assomption *
assortment	assortiment
asthmatic	asthmatique *
astrology	astrologie *
astronaut	astronaute *
atomic	atomique *
atrophy	atrophie *
attack	attaque *
audio visual	audio visuel *
august	auguste *
automatic	automatique *
autonomy	autonomie *
autopsy	autopsie *

B

English	French
baccalaureate	baccalauréat*
baggage	bagage
balloon	ballon
bamboo	bambou
banana	banane*
beauty	beauté*
baby	bebe
benign	bénigne *
biology	biologie *
blue	bleu
bomb	bombe*
brilliant	brillant
bureaucrat	bureaucrate*

C

English	French
cabin	cabine *
cacophony	cacophonie *
calamity	calamité *
calculator	calculateur *
caliber	calibre
calm	calme *
Calvary	Calvaire *
cap	cape + *
Capricorn	Capricorne *
character	caractère *
caravan	caravane *
carcass	carcasse O
cardinal	cardinal
cardiology	cardiologie *
caress	caresse O
carrot	carotte *
cartography	cartographie *
cathedral	cathédrale *
catholic	catholique *
causality	causalité *
cavalry	cavalerie *
cavern	caverne *
cavity	cavité *
celery	céleri *
censor	censeur + *
ceramic	céramique *
cereal	céréale *
ceremony	cérémonie *
chain	chaine *

chaplain	chaplin *
chapel	chapelle *
charity	charité *
charm	charme
chimney	cheminée *
chiropractor	chiropracteur *
chocolate	chocolat O *
chronology	chronologie *
cigar	cigare *
cement	ciment *
clarion	clairon
class	classe *
classic	classique *
climate	climat O *
cleavage	clivage *
cohort	cohorte *
coincidence	coïncidence *
collaborator	collaborateur *
colony	colonie *
comedy	comédie *
comet	comète *
comic	comique *
committee	comite *
command	commander *
commandment	commandement *
communism	communisme *
company	compagnie + *
compartment	compartiment
compass	compas *
compatibility	compatibilité *
compatriot	compatriote *
complete	complet O *

complex	complexe *
composer	compositeur *
concierge	concierge
conclave	conclave
condolence	condoléances *
conductor	conducteur *
confidential	confidentiel *
conform	conforme *
congress	congrès *
conjunction	conjonction *
conjugation	conjugaison *
conjugal	conjugale *
consumer	consommateur *
context	contexte *
contrast	contraste *
contraband	contrebande *
convex	convexe *
cotton	coton + *
color	couleur *
crab	crabe *
cramp	crampe *

D

English	French
debonair	débonnaire*
December	Décembre*
defensible	défendable*
degree	degré*
deliquescence	déliquescent*
demand	demande*
demilitarization	démilitarisation*
demobilization	démobilisation*
democrat	démocrate*
demography	démographie*
density	densité*
dentist	dentiste*
department	département*
dependence	dépendance*
deputy	député*
dermatology	dermatologie*
descendent	descendant*
descent	descente*
despot	despote*
detest	déteste*
diagram	diagramme*
dialect	dialecte*
dichotomy	dichotomie*
differential	différentiel*
dinosaur	dinosaure*
diplomat	diplomate*
director	directeur*
disappoint	désappointe*
disapprove	désapprouve*

disarm	désarme*
disaster	désastre *
disc	disque*
discredit	discrédite*
discreet	discret *
disorder	désordre*
distortion	distorsion*
diversity	diversité*
dividend	dividende*
doctor	docteur *
dogma	dogme
domain	domaine*
drama	drame*
dramatic	dramatique*
droll	drôle*
druid	druide*
duplicity	duplicité*
dynamic	dynamique*
dynasty	dynastie *
dysentery	dysenterie*

E

English	French
ecology	écologie *
economy	économie* +
economic	économique*
effigy	effigie*
Egypt	Egypte*
elastic	élastique*
electricity	électricité*
electronic	électronique*
embarrass	embarrasse*
energy	énergie*
envelope	enveloppe*
epilepsy	épilepsie*
epiphany	épiphanie*
error	erreur*
eternity	éternité*
excess	excès*
example	exemple *
exotic	exotique*
exterior	extérieur*

F

English	French
facility	facilité*
faculty	faculté*
fantastic	fantastique*
fascism	fascisme*
felicity	félicité*
fertility	fertilité*
firm	firme*
flame	flamme*
fluid	fluide*
fraternal	fraternel*
fraud	fraude*
fury	fureur*
future	futur O*

G

English	French
gaff	gaffe*
gallant	galant
gallop	galop*
gastric	gastrique*
gelatin	gélatine *
generic	générique*
geography	géographie*
geology	géologie*
geometry	géométrie*
germ	germe*
gigantic	gigantesque*
giraffe	girafe*
goblet	gobelet
gourd	gourde*
grain	graine*
gram	gramme *
graphic	graphique*
gravity	gravité*
gross	gros*
group	groupe*
gymnastics	gymnastique*

H

English	French
haggard	hargard
halt	halte*
hanger	hangar*
harp	harpe*
harpoon	harpon*
hexagon	hexagone*
hierarchy	hiérarchie*
homage	hommage*
honor	honneur*
humid	humide *
humility	humilité*
humorist	humoriste*
humor	humour
hydrogen	hydrogène*

I

English	French
ideology	idéologie*
idol	idole*
illicit	illicite*
implicit	implicite*
impossibility	impossibilité*
imposter	imposteur
impractical	impraticable
impressionable	impressionnable
incest	inceste*
inept	inepte*
inert	inerte*
ingrate	ingrat O *
interpreter	interprète*
intimate	intimité *
intransigence	intransigeance*
intrepid	intrépide*
invalid	invalide*
irreconcilable	irréconciliable*
irreducible	irréductible*
irresponsible	irresponsable
isle	ile*

J

English	French

NONE

K

English	French

NONE

L

English	French

NONE

M

English	French
madam	madame*
magistrate	magistrat O *
magnate	magnat O *
mandolin	mandoline*
march	marche*
marionette	marionnette* +
melody	mélodie *
metabolism	métabolisme*
method	méthode*
meter	mètre*
model	modèle*
modern	moderne*
modest	modeste*
monosyllable	monosyllabe
monotheism	monothéisme*
morbid	morbide*
multiform	multiforme*
multimillionaire	multimillionnaire
myriad	myriade *
myth	mythe*

N

English	French
nomad	nomade
norm	norme *

O

English	French
observe	observer* +
omelet	omelette*
opportunism	opportunisme*
optimism	optimisme*
organ	organe* +
organist	organiste*
orgasm	orgasme*
origin	origine*
orthodox	orthodoxe*
oval	ovale*
oxygen	oxygène *

English	French
pact	pacte*
paganism	paganisme*
palm	palme*
panther	panthère*
paradox	paradoxe*
paragraph	paragraphe*
pass	passé* +
patriarch	patriarche*
patrician	patricien*
pavilion	pavillon*
pedal	pédale*
penicillin	pénicilline*
pentagon	pentagone*
perch	perche*
period	période*
pessimism	pessimisme*
petal	pétale*
petrol	pétrole*
phonograph	phonographe*
pilot	pilote* +
placid	placide*
plain	plaine*
planet	planète*
plant	plante*
polygon	polygone*
poplin	popeline*
porcelain	porcelaine*
porter	porteur*
precept	précepte*

preexist	préexiste*
prefix	préfixe*
press	presse* +
preterit	prétérite*
pretext	prétexte *
problem	problème*
proclaim	proclame*
program	programme*
pronoun	pronom*
pro-rate	prorata*
protagonist	protagoniste*
protein	protéine*
protocol	protocole*
proverb	proverbe*
pulp	pulpe*
pylon	pilon
pyramid	pyramide*

Q

English	French
NONE	

R

English	French
ramp	rampe*
realism	réalisme*
reflex	reflexe*
reform	reforme* +
rendezvous	rendez-vous
repast	repas* +
reprimand	réprimande*
reservist	réserviste*
rest	reste*
rhubarb	rhubarbe*
rich	riche*
rigid	rigide*
ruin	ruine*
rhythm	rythme*

S

English	French
salad	salade*
sandal	sandale*
sarcasm	sarcasme*
satyr	satyre
scandal	scandale*
scepter	sceptre
schism	schisme *
schist	schiste*
sever	sévère*
sex	sexe* +
sign	signe* +
siren	sirène* +
Slav	Slave*
solid	solide*
solvent	solvant
sordid	sordide*
spasm	spasme*
specter	spectre*
sperm	sperme*
spiral	spirale*
spirit	spirite* +
stratagem	stratagème*
stupid	stupide*
subtle	subtile
suffix	suffixe*
superb	superbe*
syllogism	syllogisme*
symbol	symbole*
symptom	symptôme*
syndicate	syndicat *
synod	synode*
system	système*

T

English	French
tacit	tacite*
taciturn	taciturne*
tartar	tartare*
tavern	taverne*
tax	taxe*
technocrat	technocrate*
telegraph	télégraphe*
term	terme*
testicle	testicule
text	texte*
theorem	théorème*
thyme	thym*
thyroid	thyroïde*
timid	timide*
topaz	topaze*
torch	torche*
tourism	tourisme*
tricolor	tricolore*
triumph	triomphe*
tulip	tulipe*
typhoid	typhoïde*

U

English	French
uniform	uniforme*
unisex	unisexe*
unison	unisson*
unity	unité*
universe	univers*
university	université*
urban	urbain*
urgency	urgence * +
utility	utilité*

V

English	French
valiant	valliant*
valid	valide*
value	valeur* +
vandal	vandale*
vanity	vanité*
vapor	vapeur*
vaporize	vaporise*
vast	vaste*
vector	vecteur*
vegetarian	végétarien*
vehicle	véhicule*
vein	veine* +
velocity	vélocité*
verb	verbe*
verify	vérifie*
vermin	vermine*
victim	victime*
vinyl	vinyle*
virginity	virginité*
visit	visite*
vitamin	vitamine*
vulgar	vulgaire*

W

English	French
NONE	

X

English	French
NONE	

Y

English	French
NONE	

Z

English	French
zodiac	zodiaque*

Acknowledgments

Having procrastinated on developing this dictionary for over 10 years, I must accredit its ultimate completion to the following:

Mrs. Ball,
my French 101 professor at the
College of Marin.
Who, upon quitting her class in 1962,
I had promised to eventually
return to the task of learning to speak French.

My Spouse, Arlette,
whose maternal language was French and
has, for more than 45 years, endured
my limited and deplorable attempts to speak French.

Mr. Doug Busey,
whose instructive and patient powers in
exposing me to the merits of employing the
use of Excel systems with the development
of this Dictionary.

Webster's New World
French/English – English/French Dictionary,

in which I laboriously spent hours
reviewing in order to identify the words
referenced in this Dictionary

To these four, along with the hundreds of individuals in France that patiently endured my feeble attempts to communicate with them in French, I extend my everlasting gratitude and appreciation.

CPSIA information can be obtained
at www.ICGtesting.com
Printed in the USA
BVOW06s1940040117

472639BV00010B/88/P